977.3

Mil

10948

THE FLAT MARKET

CONCORDIA LUTHERAN

4660

Sale

D0516428

THE DAY WILL COME WHEN OUR SILENCE WILL BE MORE
POWERFUL THAN THE VOICES YOU ARE THROTTLING TODAY.

The police fought the workers at the Haymarket Riot.

977.3
1080

Cornerstones of Freedom

The Story of

THE HAYMARKET RIOT

By Charnan Simon

CHILDRENS PRESS ®

CHICAGO

CONCORDIA UNIVERSITY LIBRARY
PORTLAND, OR 97211

Circular (right), printed both in English and German, announced the time and place of the Haymarket rally (left).

Library of Congress Cataloging-in-Publication Data

Simon, Charnan.
   The story of the Haymarket Riot / by Charnan Simon.
     p.   cm. — (Cornerstones of freedom)
   Includes index.
   Summary: Traces the efforts of industrial workers to secure better
working conditions, including the eight-hour day and how
deteriorating relations between striking workers and police led to the
Haymarket Square Riot which resulted in the unfair convictions of
eight social revolutionaries in a murder-conspiracy trial.
   ISBN 0-516-04740-X
   1. Haymarket Square Riot, Chicago, Ill., 1886—Juvenile
literature. [1. Haymarket Square Riot, Chicago, Ill.,
1886. 2. Labor and laboring classes—
History.] I. Title. II. Series.
HX846.C4S46 1988   88-22803
977.3'11041-dc19   CIP
                                    AC

Children's Press®, Chicago
Copyright © 1988 by Regensteiner Publishing Enterprises, Inc.
All rights reserved. Printed in the United States of America.
Weekly Reader is a trademark of Field Publications.

Samuel Fielden

The crowd in Chicago's Haymarket Square was growing restless. For nearly three hours union speakers had been listing the hardships faced by the workers in America. Calls for shorter working hours and higher pay had been heard. Charges of police brutality against pro-union workers had been made. Now, however, a cold rain was falling, and the crowd began to break up.

By 10:30 P.M., less than 300 listeners remained. The last speaker, Samuel Fielden, was just ending his speech when it happened. Without warning, 180 policemen, led by Captain John Bonfield, marched into the crowd. They stopped three or four paces from the truck wagon that had served as a speakers' platform. Startled, Fielden stopped speaking and looked at Captain Bonfield.

After the bomb exploded, the police began shooting and the workers began running.

The captain didn't waste any time. "In the name of the people of the State of Illinois, I command this meeting immediately and peaceably to disperse." Bonfield looked challengingly at Samuel Fielden and repeated his command.

"We are peaceable," Fielden said mildly, as he began to climb down from the wagon.

It was as if a signal had been given. There was a brief, dim light and a small sputtering sound. With no other warning, a dynamite bomb was thrown from somewhere in the crowd. It exploded, killing one sergeant outright and knocking down nearly sixty other policemen.

For a moment, both the crowd and the police were frozen in horror. Then, the police opened fire. The stunned spectators came to life and began running. It was over in a matter of minutes. At least two people lay dead on the streets, and nearly a hundred more were seriously wounded. As one historian put it, the Haymarket Riot of May 4, 1886, had ended, and the Haymarket affair had begun.

Actually, the events leading up to the Haymarket Riot had begun years before. After the Civil War ended in 1865, life in America began to change. The transcontinental railroad opened up the West for increased settlement—and an increased need for manufactured goods. A steady stream of cheap immigrant labor fueled the factories of the Industrial Revolution. Vast fortunes were made by factory owners.

With these fortunes, many owners built new factories. But many of these newer factories were run by machines—and more machines working meant fewer people working. With fewer people working and earning wages, there were fewer buyers for the goods being made by machines. It was a vicious circle, and it led to economic depression.

The laborers—mostly recent European immigrants—worked long hours for low wages. It wasn't uncommon for workers—even children—to toil in a factory or mine for ten, twelve, or even fourteen hours a day. A healthy man might earn $2.00 a day, a child was lucky to bring home 70¢.

In Chicago, as in most American cities, thousands of laborers lived in poverty. The famous social worker Jane Addams described the Chicago slums in these words: "The streets are inexpressibly dirty, the number of schools inadequate, sanitary legislation unenforced, and street lighting bad." This poverty, combined with terrible working conditions, naturally led to worker unrest.

Of course, not all employers were cruel. Many treated their employees fairly. They recognized that happy, healthy employees were more productive than unhappy, exhausted ones. But, as one worker in

Jane Addams (left) devoted her life to helping the poor. Sewing piecework at home (right) was a common occupation for every member of an immigrant family.

Children in this vegetable cannery worked long hours for little pay.

1883 put it, "The employer has pretty much the same feeling toward the men that he has toward his machinery. He wants to get as much as he can out of his men at the cheapest rate. . .That is all he cares for the man generally."

The growing tide of worker unrest led to the rise of the labor-union movement. Various labor unions sprang up to fight for laws that would improve the life of the American worker. They wanted to outlaw child labor, increase hourly wages, and decrease the number of hours in a legal work day. Because these demands clashed with the interests of the factory and mine owners, conflicts often broke out between the two groups. The police were frequently called in to settle these conflicts—and when this happened it was the workers who suffered.

By 1886, the big issue was the eight-hour working day. As one labor union motto proclaimed, "Eight Hours for Work, Eight Hours for Recreation and Rest, Eight Hours for Sleep." But not all unions agreed on how to fight for the eight-hour day. Some unions, such as the Chicago-based Knights of Labor, were working to pass federal and state legislation that would legally limit the work day. Other unions, such as the Federation of Organized Trades and Labor Unions, had called for a nationwide workers' strike on May 1, 1886. Still other workers, who were members of the American Socialist Labor Party, held out for armed revolution against employers.

Workers at the Horn Brothers Bedroom Furniture Manufacturing Company were photographed in 1886 before a strike. The youngest workers are in the front sitting on the ground.

For these social revolutionaries, nothing less than a complete overhaul of the American industrial economy would do.

Although their leaders did not agree, workers across the country supported the May 1 strike. Newspapers, politicians, and business leaders were against the strike. They said the eight-hour day would encourage "loafing and gambling, rioting, debauchery, and drunkenness." Employers warned that striking workers would be fired and that new workers, called "scabs" by the strikers, would be hired in their places.

As worker support for the May 1 strike mounted, local police forces around the country geared up for battle. Everyone assumed that violence would go hand in hand with the strikes.

When May 1 finally dawned, workers in every major industrial center laid down their tools and went on strike. Over 350,000 workers in Milwaukee, St. Louis, Cincinnati, Washington, Baltimore, New York, Philadelphia, Boston, and Chicago demonstrated for the eight-hour day. The strike was strongest in Chicago, supported by 80,000 machinists, plumbers, brickmakers, freight-handlers, printers, stockyard employees, toymakers, plasterers, and other workers.

But despite these numbers, the strike day was

fairly quiet. There were no major clashes with police or employers. In Chicago, a gala ball closed the day of peaceful demonstrations and parades. Citizens all over the city breathed a sigh of relief.

But the troubles weren't over yet. Despite the gains made by the strikers—some 185,000 workers nationwide were granted shorter hours—many employers stubbornly refused to deal with the strikers. One such employer was the McCormick Harvesting Machine factory on Chicago's west side. This factory had long been a source of labor disputes. Since February of 1886, the plant had been shut down, and employees (who had fought with management over their right to join in union activities) had been locked out. In March, the plant had opened again, this time manned by some 300 non-union "scabs."

For the next two months, there were frequent clashes between the striking workers, the scabs, and the police. Finally, on May 3, things came to a head. Some 500 strikers met the scabs as they left the plant, using sticks and stones to drive them back into the factory. The police were called. A detail of 200 soon arrived, firing without warning into the crowd of strikers. One man was killed, five or six were wounded by bullets, and many more were seriously injured by the policemen's clubs.

Newspapers showed strikers attacking police at the McCormick factory (left) and fighting scabs at the Chicago Burlington and Quincy Railroad (right).

The reaction by Chicago's labor organizers was swift. August Spies, a social revolutionary, printed up a circular urging workers to "arm" themselves and appear "in full force" at a protest meeting in Haymarket Square the following night. In a later circular, Spies took off the words "To arms!" fearing that the threat of violence would both attract too much police attention and, more importantly, frighten people away from the rally.

CONCORDIA LUTHERAN SCHOOL
4663 Lancaster Drive NE
Salem, Oregon 97305
503/393-7188

August Spies   Albert Parsons

When Spies arrived in Haymarket Square the evening of May 4, the meeting had not yet started. He spoke to the crowd of some 1,200 spectators. "Gentlemen and fellow workmen...this meeting was called for the purpose of discussing the general situation of the eight-hour workday strike, and the events which have taken place in the last forty-eight hours. It seems to have been the opinion of the authorities that this meeting was called for the purpose of raising a little row and disturbance. This, however, was not the intention of the committee that called the meeting..."

Spies talked about the McCormick riot and the rights and responsibilities of the American worker. Around nine o'clock, he turned the speaker's stand over to Albert Parsons. Parsons, another social revolutionary, talked about the conditions of the American working man and woman.

By the time Samuel Fielden was introduced, the rain had begun and the crowd was leaving. Among those to leave early was Chicago Mayor Carter H. Harrison. Finding no signs of agitation or violence, Harrison left shortly after Fielden began to speak. On his way home, Harrison stopped at the nearby Desplaines Street police station. He reported that the meeting was peaceful and recommended that the police (who had been on stand-by alert) be "released for their ordinary duties."

But Police Captain Bonfield chose to ignore this recommendation. Shortly after the mayor left the station, Bonfield and his men marched on Haymarket Square. The meeting was halted, the bomb was thrown, and the Haymarket affair began.

The next day Chicago—and indeed the entire nation—was in an uproar. Newspapers accused

Carter Harrison

John Bonfield

Spies, Parsons, and Fielden of throwing the bomb—even though Parsons had already left the meeting by the time the bomb exploded. Sensational newspaper headlines fanned the flames of hysteria. "Anarchy's Red Hand!" screamed the *New York Times* on May 5. "Rioting and Bloodshed in the Streets of Chicago—Police Mowed Down with Dynamite!" The next day's paper condemned "the Anarchist's murder of policemen in Chicago" and hoped the "cowardly savages who plotted and carried out this murder shall suffer the death they deserve."

Other newspapers reported that the Haymarket Riot—and indeed other labor-related disturbances—were the work of foreign-born anarchists and socialists. They called for swift punishment of the "revolutionaries." There was no question of waiting until all the facts were in. In the eyes of the American public, Spies, Parsons, Fielden, and their socialist brothers were guilty of murder.

Though labor unions everywhere condemned the bomb throwing, the labor movement as a whole, and the eight-hour movement in particular, suffered by association. As one editorial put it, "No doubt the workmen on strike in Chicago mean what they say in denouncing the ruffians who have used the name of 'labor' as a pretext for murder. They would prove their sincerity still more completely if they were to abandon, for the present, their demand for a change in their hours of work. . ."

Few newspapers maintained any objectivity. One was the labor journal *John Swinton's Paper*. This journal pointed out that, had the squad of armed police not charged on the meeting, it would probably have ended peacefully enough on its own. It went on to say that, although there was no justification for bomb throwing, there *was* justification for the workers' dissatisfactions. Hysteria over the bloodshed shouldn't blind people to the desirability of an eight-hour workday.

The *Labor Enquirer* noted that "Twice as many honest men may be murdered in a coal mine as have been killed in Chicago, and there isn't any noise at all about it. The American press is a wonderfully lopsided affair."

And the *Topeka Citizen* pointed out that perhaps the way to stop socialist and anarchist riots was to erase the working and living conditions that brought about workers' discontent.

But these few voices were barely heard. The press and the public alike called for revenge.

And revenge was swift in coming. Within days, hundreds of workers were arrested in Chicago. The police officer in charge of these arrests was Michael J. Schaack. Captain Schaack performed his job with

On the night of the riot the wounded police officers were carried to the Desplaines Street police station (right). Michael Schaack (left) was in charge of the Haymarket investigation.

energy and imagination—perhaps too much imagination. He discovered bombs, secret societies, and conspiracies wherever he looked. As Chief of Police Ebersold said later:

It was my policy to quiet matters down as soon as possible after the 4th of May. The general unsettled state of things was an injury to Chicago. . .Captain Schaack wanted to keep things stirring. He wanted bombs to be found here, there, all around. . .I thought people would. . .sleep better if they were not afraid. . .but this man Schaack. . .wanted none of that policy. Now, here is something the public does not know. After we got the anarchist societies broken up, Schaack wanted to send out men to organize new societies right away. . .He wanted to keep the thing boiling, keep himself prominent before the public. Well, I sat down on that. . .and, of course, Schaack didn't like it. After I heard all that, I began to think there was perhaps not so much to all this anarchist business as they claimed, and I believe I was right."

Captain Schaak continued to investigate. Homes and offices were broken into and searched without warrants. Suspects were beaten or bribed into acting as witnesses. Of the hundreds of workers arrested, eight were finally brought to trial: Albert Parsons, August Spies, Samuel Fielden, Michael Schwab, Adolph Fischer, George Engel, Louis Lingg, and Oscar Neebe. Of these, only three—Parsons, Spies, and Fielden—had actually been at Haymarket Square on May 4. The rest were arrested because they were part of Chicago's radical socialist movement.

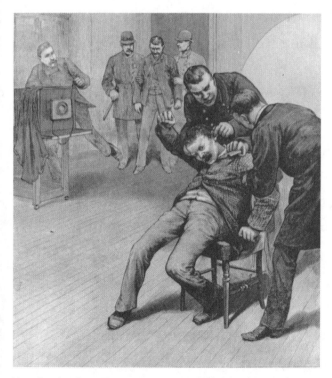

Hundreds of workers were arrested (above) and charged with such crimes as murder and inciting riot. Arrest orders, such as one issued for Rudolph Schnaukelt (right), were signed by Frederick Ebersold.

The grand jury officially accused the eight men of the murder of Mathias J. Degan, the police sergeant who was killed outright. None of the eight had been seen anywhere near the bomb—the actual bomb thrower never was identified. Nonetheless, Spies, Parsons, and the others were to be tried as murderers, on the grounds that their speeches and ideas had influenced this unknown bomb thrower.

By the time the trial began on June 21, public opinion was, if anything, even more strongly biased against the accused. Five more policemen had died as a result of the bombing, and citizens were demanding an eye-for-an-eye vengeance. The eight were to be found guilty to set an example. Their trial would demonstrate that American institutions were stronger than any "foreign" revolutionary ideas. (Of the eight accused, all but Parsons and Fielden were either German-born or of German descent.)

With public sentiment running so strongly against the accused, it was no surprise that their trial was anything but fair. The trouble began with the selection of the jury. The jury was not chosen in the usual way, by drawing random names from a box. Instead, Judge Joseph E. Gary appointed a special bailiff, Henry L. Ryce, to select jury members. Technically, this was legal. And if Ryce had been fair, an unbiased jury might still have been selected. But

Ryce believed the eight were guilty. More than once he was heard to say, "I am managing this case, and know what I am about. Those fellows are going to be hanged as certain as death."

It was easy for Ryce to present only those men who agreed with him. When the defense lawyers protested this prejudiced selection, Judge Gary repeatedly overruled them. Of the twelve men finally

Haymarket Riot Trial

The members of the jury (left) and the defendants (right)

The Haymarket trial began in the courtroom of Judge Gary on June 21, 1887.

chosen, all admitted to having already formed opinions about the guilt of the accused men. Nine of the jury were against socialism. One was a relative of a bomb victim. And not one juror was a laborer or member of a union.

And so the trial began. There was a mild stir on the first day. Albert Parsons, who had been in hiding since May 5, unexpectedly appeared in court and turned himself in to be tried with his friends. Perhaps he felt that this sign of confidence in his own innocence would work in the defendants' favor. If so, he was sadly mistaken.

From the beginning, the judge and jury were against the defendants. Judge Gary refused defense counsel Captain William P. Black's motion to have the eight tried individually. The judge also limited Captain Black's right to cross-examine State witnesses—many of whom were either policemen, or paid by the police to give prejudicial testimony. State's Attorney Julius Grinnell, on the other hand, could ask whatever questions that he wished. Grinnell repeatedly referred to the defendants' "inflammatory" statements about violence. But Black was never allowed to clarify these statements, or to show that the defendants only advocated the use of arms for self-defense.

Throughout the trial, the police displayed all types of dynamite and bombs to frighten the jury and imply that these were the everyday weapons of the accused. No proof was offered that the defendants threw, planted, or even knew about the Haymarket bomb. No proof was offered that Spies, Parsons, or Fielden had encouraged the crowd to

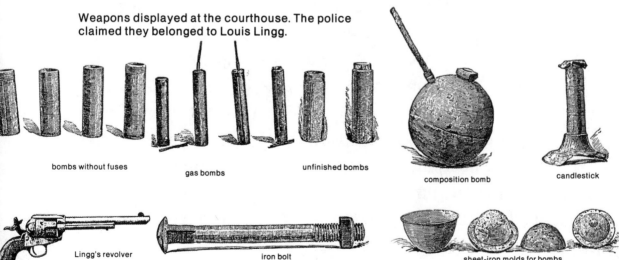

Weapons displayed at the courthouse. The police claimed they belonged to Louis Lingg.

bombs without fuses

gas bombs

unfinished bombs

composition bomb

candlestick

Lingg's revolver

iron bolt

sheet-iron molds for bombs

violence in their speeches—even Mayor Harrison testified that their speeches seemed "tame." No proof was offered that violence of any sort was ever planned—as the defense pointed out, would Parsons have his wife and two children with him at Haymarket if he knew about the bomb?

From the beginning, it was evident that the eight men were not just accused of murdering a policeman. They were on trial for their political ideas. They all, to one extent or another, were involved with the socialist labor movement in Chicago. Only three had been present at the Haymarket meeting; the rest hadn't even known about it. Oscar Neebe's only crime seemed to be that he owned two dollars' worth of stock in a socialist newspaper and kept a red flag and a pistol in his home. As one of the defendants was to say later, "I am condemned to die for writing newspaper articles and making speeches."

And so the trial ground to an end. The defense counsel's closing arguments fell on deaf ears. As one juror said later, "We had already made up our minds. . .to convict every one of the prisoners." Clearly, the jury supported State's Attorney Grinnell's closing speech: "Law is on trial. Anarchy is on trial. These men have been selected, picked out by the grand jury and indicted because they were leaders. They are no more guilty than the thousands

Entered according to Act of Congress in the year 1887, by PAUL J. MORAND, in the Office of the Librarian of Congress, at Washington.

PRINCIPALS IN THE HAYMARKET RIOT,

Chicago, 1886.

GEO. INGHAM,   JULIUS S. GRINNELL,   Judge JOS. E. GARY.   Capt. WM. P. BLACK,   WM. A. FOSTER,
Attorney.   State's Attorney.   Attorney   Attorney.

Capt. WM. BUCKLEY   Capt. MICHAEL SCHAACK. FREDRICK EBERSOLD,   JOHN BONFIELD.   Capt. WM. WARD.
        Capt. A. W. HATHAWAY,   Chief of Police.   Inspector of Police Capt. SIMON O'DONNELL.

ALB'T R. PARSONS.   AUG. SPIES.   LOUIS LINGG.   SAM'L FIELDEN.   ADOLPH FISCHER.   MICH'L SCHWAB.   GEO. ENGEL.   OSCAR W. NEEBE.

who follow them. Gentlemen of the jury: convict these men, make examples of them, hang them and you save our institutions, our society."

If there had been any doubt in the jurors' minds about the guilt of the accused, Judge Gary's final instructions erased it. He informed the jury that the defendants could be found guilty "beyond a reasonable doubt" of influencing the bomb thrower—even though that person was never identified. Years later, Judge Gary said, "If I had a little strained the law...I was to be commended for so doing."

At ten o'clock on the morning of August 20, the jury marched into the courtroom with their verdict.

Political cartoonists wanted the Haymarket defendants to receive the death sentence.

Solemnly, the jury foreman began to read: "We the jury find the defendants, Adolph Spies, Michael Schwab, Samuel Fielden, Albert Parsons, Adolph Fischer, George Engel, and Louis Lingg guilty of murder...and fix the penalty at death. We find the defendant Oscar Neebe guilty of murder...and fix the penalty at imprisonment...for fifteen years."

The courtroom erupted, as newspaper reporters rushed out. The crowd on the sidewalk outside the Criminal Court Building burst into cheers. Proposals were made to offer the jury members a cash reward for coming to the "right" decision. Only the defendants, their families, and their lawyers seemed stunned by the decision.

Later, Captain Black said,

"I was never so shocked in all my experience. . .I should not have been more horrified had I myself received the death sentence. I had expected a conviction, of course. But seven men convicted to hang! We did not expect an acquittal from a jury so prejudiced, but such a verdict as this destroys a good deal of my faith in human nature. Mr. Grinnell had in his closing argument placed the defendants in the order in which he considered them guilty, beginning with Spies and ending with Neebe, and any ordinary jury would have seen from that that he did not expect a conviction in all cases."

Press and public around the nation hailed the jury's decision as just, righteous, and wise. The only regret was that, because of the death sentence, the men were automatically entitled to an appeal.

Shaken though they were, the defense lawyers immediately began their application for this appeal. And on March 13, 1887, the six judges of the Illinois Supreme Court met in Ottawa to further consider the appeal.

The Supreme Court noted that the Haymarket trial hadn't been entirely fair. The justices pointed out the ways in which the men had been denied their rights, but those same justices still upheld the lower court's decision!

The defense appealed the case to the United States Supreme Court, but the court refused to review the case.

The last hope was an appeal to the governor for pardon. By now, public opinion had softened. Most

Americans still supported the verdict. But a growing minority of voices could be heard in support of the eight condemned men.

Labor organizations, at first afraid to associate themselves with the eight, began to come out strongly in favor of a pardon. They were joined by a number of prominent American lawyers, judges, writers, and intellectuals. The noted novelist William Dean Howells wrote a letter of appeal to Illinois Governor Oglesby and urged others to follow his example. Howells said, "I have never believed them guilty of murder, or of anything but their opinions. . .I beseech you to. . .do what one great and blameless man may do to arrest the greatest wrong that ever threatened our fame as a nation."

As the November 11 execution date drew nearer, Oglesby was bombarded with letters and petitions urging a pardon. On November 9 he held a public hearing, at which he heard dozens of appeals and reviewed mountains of paperwork. For every person who urged mercy, another stood up to insist that Oglesby do nothing to change the court's decision.

November 11 dawned with no pardons forthcoming. But there was other sensational news—Louis Lingg had cheated the hangman by committing suicide in his cell. Barely had this shocking knowledge sunk in when the governor issued his

long-awaited statement. The death sentences of Samual Fielden and Michael Schwab were commuted to life imprisonment.

Spies, Fischer, Parsons, and Engel accepted their death sentence calmly. "The fortitude they displayed," wrote the *Chicago Tribune*, "was worthy of a better cause. In a righteous contest. . .they might have been heroes."

At 11:30 A.M. on November 11, the four men were led to the gallows. As the nooses were lowered, Spies' voice rang out: "There will come a time when our silence will be more powerful than the voices you strangle today!" This was quickly followed by Parsons' plea, "Will I be allowed to speak, O men of America? Let the voice of the people be heard!"

Then the trap was sprung, and an episode in American history was brought to a close.

Or was it? As many as fifteen thousand people attended the executed men's funeral in Waldheim Cemetery, where a monument to their martyrdom was erected in 1893. Their deaths did not end their influence, just as their executions did not cripple the labor movement they all supported. The eight-hour working day did, in fact, become law in America, and the men who died for their beliefs have become heroes instead of murderers.

There was one final bit of controversy surrounding the eight convicted men. On June 26, 1893, the Governor of Illinois, John P. Altgeld, issued a pardon for all eight men. Altgeld was a man of independence, courage, and integrity. After reviewing the court records he came to the conclusion that all of

The burial at Waldheim Cemetery (left) did not end the Haymarket affair. Governor John P. Altgeld (right) pardoned all eight defendants on June 26, 1893.

the defendants were completely innocent. Altgeld bluntly declared that the jurists were incompetent, the judge's rulings illegal, and the evidence completely insufficient to convict any of the men.

Needless to say, Altgeld's pardon stirred up a storm of controversy. There were those who claimed it would ruin his political career (it didn't—but when Altgeld was warned of this, he replied, "If I decide they were innocent I will pardon them, by God, no matter what happens to my career!"). There were those who said he was right to pardon the men, but he shouldn't have criticized the original court in doing so. There were those who applauded the decision wholeheartedly—and, of course, there were those who condemned it bitterly.

But Altgeld braved the storm and stood firm by his decision. Fielden, Schwab, and Neebe were released from prison, and the five dead men had the stigma of guilt removed from their names.

No one ever discovered who actually threw the Haymarket bomb. But its explosion had an international effect. Today May 1, the day originally set aside to call attention to the eight-hour working day, is celebrated as the most important workers' holiday in the world. From Chicago's west side to an international workers' holiday—all by way of Haymarket Square.

Both sides erected monuments to those who died because of the Haymarket Riot. The police monument (left) now stands before police headquarters. The worker's memorial (right) stands in Waldheim-Forest Homes Cemetery.

PHOTO CREDITS

Chicago Historical Society—1, 8 (left), 10, 13 (left),
    14, 15 (left), 18 (left), 19 (right), 25, 30 (right),
    32 (left)
Culver Picture Service—5, 6, 18 (right)
Bettman Archive—4 (left)
Historical Picture Service—2, 4 (right), 13 (right),
    19 (left), 21 (left), 22, 26, 29, 30 (left)
Charles Kerr Publishing—21 (right), 23, 32 (right)
Illinois Labor History Society—15 (right)
Granger Collection—8 (right), 9
Cover: Chuck Hills

About the Author

   Charnan Simon grew up reading anything she could get her hands on in Ohio, Georgia, Oregon, and Washington. She holds a B.A. in English Literature from Carleton College in Northfield, Minnesota, and an M.A. in English Literature from the University of Chicago. She worked in children's trade books after college and then went on to become the managing editor of *Cricket* magazine before beginning her career as a freelance author. Ms. Simon has written dozens of books and articles for young people and especially likes writing—and reading—history, biography, and fiction of all sorts.

Weekly Reader Books offers several exciting
card and activity programs. For information,
write to WEEKLY READER BOOKS, P.O. Box 16636,
Columbus, Ohio 43216.

C.Lit HX 846 .C4 S46 1988
Simon, Charnan.
The story of the Haymarket
    Riot

CONCORDIA LU...
   4663 Lanca...
   Salem, Or...
   503/393-7188

SIMON, HARNAN
HAYMARKET RIOT, THE

   977.3
BOOK   1080-A

CONCORDIA LUTHERAN SCHOOL
   4663 Lancaster Drive NE
   Salem, Oregon 97305
        503/393-7188